Pigs in Mud

Written by Michèle Dufresne

PIONEER VALLEY EDUCATIONAL PRESS, INC.

The pigs sit in the mud.

Pigs love mud. It helps them cool off because pigs don't sweat like humans.

The pigs **nap** in the sun.

Pigs rest a lot during the day. They nap in the sun to stay warm or in the shade to stay cool.

4

I can see **tags** on the pigs.

Pigs on farms wear tags in their ears. The tag has a number so the farmer knows which pig is which.

The pig digs.

Pigs use their snouts to dig in the dirt. They sniff out bugs, roots, and other treats under the ground.

The pig can get bugs.

I see pigs in the **pens.**

nap

tags

pens

12